When Daddy Prays

Written by **Nikki Grimes**

Illustrated by **Tim Ladwig**

Published 2002 by Eerdmans Books for Young Readers
An imprint of Wm. B. Eerdmans Publishing Company
255 Jefferson S.E., Grand Rapids, Michigan 49503
P.O. Box 163, Cambridge CB3 9PU U.K.

02 03 04 05 06 07 08   7 6 5 4 3 2 1

Library of Congress Cataloging-in-Publication Data
Grimes, Nikki.
When Daddy prays / written by Nikki Grimes ; illustrated by Tim Ladwig.   p. cm.
In this collection of poems, a child expresses love and affection for Daddy
and reflects on the many times Daddy talks to God.
ISBN 0-8028-5152-5 (alk. paper)
1.Fathers—Juvenile poetry. 2. Children's poetry, American.
3. Christian poetry, American.
4. Prayer—Juvenile poetry. [1. Fathers—Poetry.
2. Prayer—Poetry. 3. Christian life—Poetry.
4. Afro-Americans—Poetry. 5. American poetry.]
I. Ladwig, Tim, ill. II. Title.
PS3557.R489982W47 2002
811'.54—dc21   99-041459

The illustrations were rendered with an underpainting of gouache,
a clear gesso base, and oil paint.
The type was set in Goudy Old Style.
Book design by Jesi Josten.

For my grandfather, Rev. Noah Grimes, a man of prayer.
— N. G.

To Dan, with thanks for your encouragement and inspired suggestions.
— T. L.

A Father's Prayer

May my children see
beyond my muscles
to your strength.

May they find
across my broad shoulders
the imprint of your wings.

May they feel your love
in the hollow
of my hand.

May they hear your voice
in the echo
of my words.

When Daddy Prays

When Daddy prays
his muscled shoulders shake.
His lips become all trembly.
And some nights I awake
because I hear
tears in his voice
when Daddy prays.

When Daddy prays
my fear of darkness disappears
and angels tiptoe down the hall.
I hear them through the door and wall.
They whisper in a velvet *hussssshhh*
that floats me off to sleep
when Daddy prays.

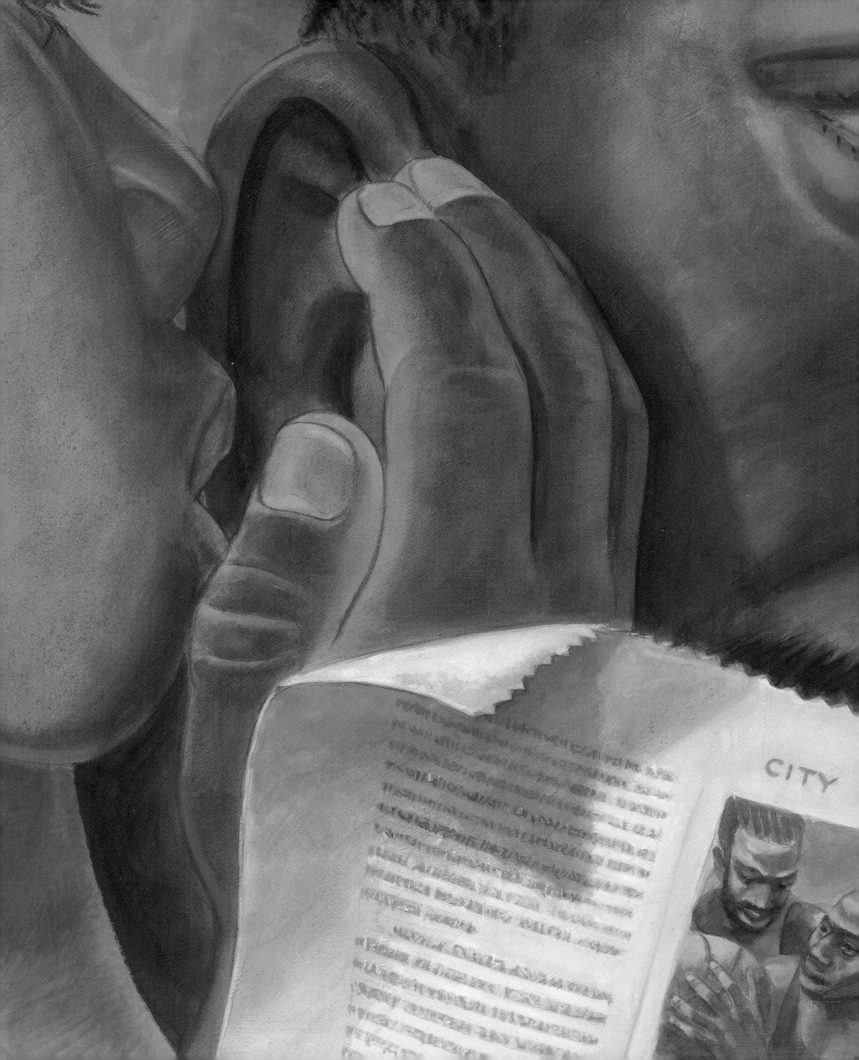

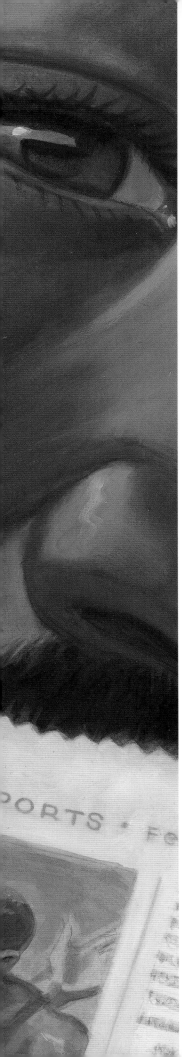

Daddy Says

Daddy says
you rock him
in your arms
the way he
once rocked me.
That after he
tucks me in
and switches
off the light,
he whispers
secrets to you
through the night
exactly like
I whisper mine
to him.
But yesterday
I think
I heard him say
you're a better
listener.

Like Him

I tip Daddy's hat back so I can see
to roll his shirtsleeves like donuts.
Even so, the stripes swallow
my arms down to my wrists.

His pants would puddle at my ankles
if I didn't tie a rope around my waist.
But that's okay.
They'll fit me one day.

I shuffle down the hall, my small feet like
tugboats dragging the ships of his shoes.
Daddy turns from the altar,
smiles, and waves me over.

I hurry to him, drop to my knees
and kneel in his shadow.
I already know what to say —
"Our Father, whose heart is heaven . . . "

Baby Brother

They sent him home half-finished,
still scrunched up
like a brown package.

They should've ironed him out first,
if you ask me. But Daddy
doesn't seem to notice.

Last night, he leaned over that
wrinkled creature in the bib,
sleeping in what used to be my crib.

"Make me a godly man," he said.
"Help me show this little one
exactly how it's done."

I punched my pillow, jealous as could be
'til Daddy asked the Lord
to please watch over *me*.

Home Run

The pitcher stabs
the ground with
a sneakered toe,
rocks back,
cranks his arm,
and *whooossh!*
throws a fast,
hard stare. His
snarling lips dare
me to step up
to the plate, but
I don't scare easy.
I grip that bat
like it's a branch
and I'm the tree
and we are one,
and I hear my
daddy's cries rise
from the stands —
"*Rip* a line drive!
Smash a grounder!
Go, batter!
Go, batter!
Go — *Sweet Jesus!*
Sail that ball
over the wall!"

Lost and Found

He felt inside his pockets.
He checked the dresser drawer.
He peeked beneath the sofa
and felt around the floor.

I offered my assistance
when I found him on his knees
muttering to himself about
a set of missing keys.

So why did he start laughing
when I told him what to do?
"Ask God to help you find it —
like you always tell *me* to."

Earth Angel

Daddy said
he needed my help,
said nobody
can weed like me,
and he's right.
Even Grandma says,
"That boy's got
the touch."
So I hopped
in the truck
and rode with him
'cross town to
old Mrs. Haynes' house.
I did my
expert weed-pulling
in her yard
while Daddy pruned
her apricot sapling
and trimmed
her bushes
and manicured
her lawn.
He paused
halfway through
the job,
turned his face
to the sun,
and mumbled
something.

"What's that,
Daddy?"
I asked.
"I was just
giving thanks,"
he said. "It's not
every day
a man's got
good health,
and good work,
and a good
weed-puller
at his side."
I grinned,
yanked another
stubborn dandelion
from the dirt,
and thanked
the Gardener
for giving me
the touch.

Confession

I scarred
the kitchen tile with mud,
it's true.

I cranked
the TV volume high,
and maybe slammed
the screen door once
or twice.

But what
does all that have to do
with rollerblades
left lonely in
the hall?

Did you
trip over them, again,
and fall?

Is that
what makes you
grind your teeth
and glare at me and shout
"God! Please!"

Is that
what the fuss is about?
You need to pray for patience, Dad.
Jesus wouldn't get
this mad.

Lessons in Grace

I

For rice
and beans
and turnip greens,
for rugged hope
and sturdy limbs —
these calloused hands
and grateful hymns
we raise.

II

Mom made oxtail soup for supper
like she did the other night,
oxtail soup with peas and carrots
like we ate the other night.
I got a whiff of oxtail
but there was no meat in sight.

I started to complain,
but Daddy stilled me with a look.
I muttered and I moaned
'til Daddy chilled me with that look.
"Lord," he said, "we thank you —
like you taught us in your book."

Bus Stop

He paced along
the yellow line
of the bus stop,
pretending patience
and faking calm.
But his eyes, half shut,
and his trembling lips
silently saying,
"Jesus, Jesus, Jesus,"
warned anyone watching
that he was sick
with worry
and might explode with it
at any moment.
"Hi, Daddy!" I called,
hopping off
the No. 2 bus.
"Sorry I'm late, but — "
My mumbled excuses
were cut short
because he swung
me in the air,
held me there
safe in time,
whispering,
"Thank you, Lord.
Thank you."

Hot Head

In our house, Monday nights are holy as Sunday.
At least, that's what you'd think the way Daddy

makes us tiptoe in and out of the living room
while he coaches TV football from an easy chair.

But last night, I didn't care about touchdowns
or passes. My head was on fire and I ran into

the room, scrambled up on Daddy's knee and
clutched him, moaning, hoping he had water

to put out the blaze. And he did, 'cause in the
sudden hush, he laid hands on me and whispered,

"Father, have mercy."

December Morning

Daddy takes his
early morning post
at the window.
Worry lines
his walnut brow.

He bows his head,
skips the small talk, and
quietly ticks off the
troubles that litter our
street like broken glass.

He asks God to meet
me at the corner, wielding
an invisible broom to sweep
aside whatever dangerous
slivers I might miss.

Unseen, I linger near
Daddy's bedroom door,
hear him blasting
this day's evil
in Jesus' name.

Then I rush outside,
laughing off the
winter's chill,
feeling warm and
fearless.

Watch Night

I yawn and fidget in the pew,
hypnotized by candlelight,
counting down the final minutes
of this year's final night.

My eyelids flutter, chasing sleep.
I fight to lift my drooping chin.
The organist tunes up the pipes
as the faithful trickle in.

At twelve o'clock, my father kneels
to consecrate the coming year
with psalms of praise and prayers of hope
left ringing in God's ear.